$$\cos x = \frac{A}{H}$$

$$\tan x = \frac{O}{A}$$

$$\frac{1}{2} \times \frac{3}{4} = \frac{3}{8}$$

WATER
SCIENCE
TRICKS

Copyright 1998 by The Child's World, Inc.
All rights reserved. No part of this book may be reproduced or utilized in any form
or by any means without written permission from the publisher.

Library of Congress Cataloging-in-Publication Data

Murray, Peter, 1952 Sept. 29
  Professor Solomon Snickerdoodle Looks at Water / author, Peter Murray :
Penny Dann, illustrator.
    p. cm.
  ISBN 1-56766-081-9
  Summary: Professor Snickerdoodle explains now to perform various float and
using drop of water as a magnifying glass.
    1. Water—Juvenile literature. [1. Water—Experiments. 2. Experiments.
3. Scientific recreations.] I. Title. II. Title: Water science tricks.
GB662.3.M87 1998
532'.0078—DC20   98-1322
                                                          CIP
                                                          AC

I ♥ SCIENCE

THE PROFESSOR'S AMAZING LIQUID

One afternoon I decided to visit my good friend, Professor Solomon Snickerdoodle. When he answered his door, I could tell he was excited.

"I have just made a Remarkable Discovery, my young friend!" he exclaimed.

"Did you find your missing socks?" I asked. The professor is always losing socks. He has the world's largest collection of unmatched socks.

"Even more Remarkable!" the professor declared. "I have identified what I believe to be the Most Important Substance on Earth."

"Would that be chocolate chip cookie dough?" I guessed, hoping that the professor would get the hint and bring out the cookies and milk.

"Even more astounding than that!" he exclaimed. "Come into my laboratory and I'll show you!"

I followed the professor inside. On his lab table sat a large glass jar.

"This," said the professor, "is **IT!**"

"A glass jar?"

"Not the jar! Its *contents*!"

I examined the jar. It was filled with a clear liquid.

"It looks like water," I said.

The professor smiled. "That," he said, "is Exactly, Precisely, Indisputably correct."

I asked, "What's so remarkable about water? I mean, unless you're thirsty, or you need a bath."

But the professor wasn't listening. He was busy setting up one of his famous experiments.

THE FLOATING NEEDLE

"First, I fill this special bowl with my magic liquid," said the professor.

"You mean, you fill a soup bowl with water," I said.

"Precisely," the professor replied. "Next, I take this steel rod . . ."

"You mean that needle?"

"Of course! It's made of steel, and it's shaped like a long, thin rod, so what's the difference?"

I had to admit that the needle was, in fact, a small steel bar. The professor carefully set the needle on the surface of the water—and there it stayed!

"A floating steel rod!" I exclaimed. "How did you do it?"

"It was easy," said the professor.

HOW TO MAKE A NEEDLE FLOAT:

Start with a clean bowl of plain, ordinary water. Hold a needle very close to the water's surface and let go. Sometimes you have to try this a few times before you can make it work. Another way to do it is to balance the needle on the tines of a fork and s-l-o-w-l-y lower it to the surface of the water. If it doesn't work at first, don't give up!

HOW IT WORKS:

Have you ever seen water bugs running across the surface of a pond? Water has a quality called surface tension that acts like a thin "skin." Surface tension is what holds water drops together. You can see this "skin" if you carefully fill a water glass all the way to the top. If you add the water very, very slowly, the water will rise higher than the top of the glass! Surface tension holds the water together.

WHY BOATS FLOAT

"**I**s surface tension what makes boats float?" I asked.

The professor shook his head. "Boats are too big to be held up by surface tension," he said. "Let me show you something."

I followed the professor into his back yard, where he showed me a small, inflatable swimming pool full of water. A Ping-Pong ball, a block of wood, and a jar top were floating on top of the water. Underneath the water, on the bottom of the pool, I could see a rock, a clamshell, and a penny.

"As you can see," said the professor, "some things float."

"Everybody knows that," I said.

The professor raised his eyebrows. "Oh, really? Then how do you explain this?" He reached out and pushed the floating jar top under the water. It quickly sank to the bottom. Then he picked the clamshell out of the pool, shook the water out of it, and set it on the water's surface. The clamshell floated.

The professor said, "As you can see, some things float some of the time. It's all a matter of *displacement.*"

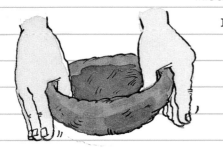

He held out a ball of modeling clay. "Do you think this ball of clay will float?"

"Of course not . . ." I said.

"Wrong again!" declared the professor. He quickly formed the ball of clay into the shape of a bowl and set it on the water. The clay bowl . . . floated!

WHY IT WORKS:

To float, an object must weigh less than the amount of water it displaces or pushes out of the way. When you drop a ball of clay into the water, it displaces an amount of water equal to its volume. Because clay weighs more than water, the ball of clay sinks. But when you make the clay into a bowl shape and set it on the water, it pushes a larger amount of water aside. If the clay weighs less than the amount of water it displaces, the bowl will float! That's why lighter objects like the Ping-Pong ball float higher in the water than heavy objects like the block of wood—because the Ping-Pong ball is lighter, it does not have to displace as much water to float.

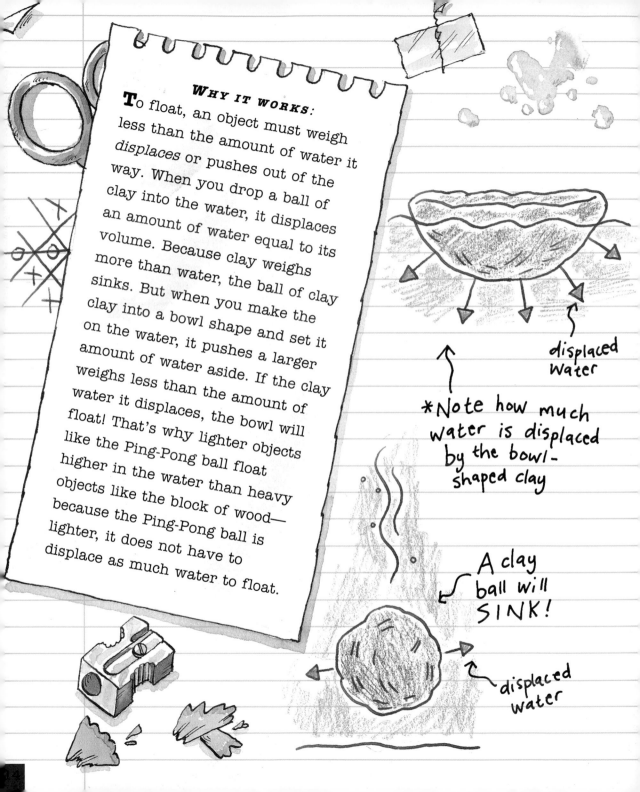

displaced water

↑

*Note how much water is displaced by the bowl-shaped clay

A clay ball will SINK!

displaced water

The ping-pong ball needs to displace only a small amount of water in order to float

The block of wood is heavier and must displace more water

"That is very confusing, Professor," I said. "Maybe we should take a cookie break and you can tell me more."

The professor shook his head. "I want to show you my new magnifier before it disappears."

THE WATER-DROP MAGNIFIER

The professor's magnifier was on his laboratory table. It looked like a piece of waxed paper with a drop of water on it. The professor set it down on a book that had some

VERY TINY WRITING LIKE THIS.

"Now look through the water drop at the writing," said the professor.

The writing was bigger when I looked through the water droplet!

VERY TINY WRITING LIKE THIS.

"Why does it do that?" I asked.

The professor smiled and turned to his blackboard.

WHY IT WORKS:

Two things are happening here.
1. *Surface tension gives the water drop its shape.*
2. *Refraction bends the light so that things look bigger. The water drop bends light like the glass lens in a magnifying glass. It spreads out the light to make tiny things look bigger.*

There are two problems with the water-drop magnifier. You can't turn it sideways or the water will run off the paper! And if you don't use it right away, the water drop will disappear.

"Disappear?" I asked.

"Yes. It will *evaporate.*"

"You mean like when a puddle dries up?"

"Exactly!" said the professor. "Evaporation is a wonderful thing! Would you care for a glass of milk?"

THE FLOWERPOT REFRIGERATOR

I wasn't sure what a glass of milk had to do with evaporation, but I was thirsty. The professor poured a glass of milk from a pitcher and handed it to me. I took a sip, but the milk was warm!

"I'd rather have my milk cold," I told him.

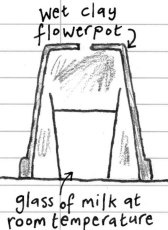

wet clay flowerpot

glass of milk at room temperature

"Of course you would, my young friend! What you need is Professor Solomon Snickerdoodle's Amazing Evaporation Refrigerator!" And with that, he took a clean, empty clay flowerpot and dunked it in a sink full of water. He poured the water out, then turned the wet flowerpot upside down over the glass of milk.

"Now we wait for one hour," he said. "Would you like to help me make some cookies?"

I'm *always* in the mood for
cookies. We mixed up a batch of
dough, stirred in a cup of
chocolate chips, and popped
the cookies into the hot oven.
Soon, we had a tray full of hot,
fresh, chocolate chip cookies.

"How about a glass of milk?"
asked the professor.

"*Cold* milk?"

The professor lifted the wet
flowerpot off the glass of milk. I
took a sip. The milk was cold!

How to make an Evaporation Refrigerator:

All you need for this is a clean clay flowerpot and some water. Be sure to use a *plain clay flowerpot*—not the kind with a shiny, decorated surface. Soak it in water for a few minutes, then turn it upside down. After a few minutes you can feel the flowerpot getting cold. Whatever you put inside will get cold, too!

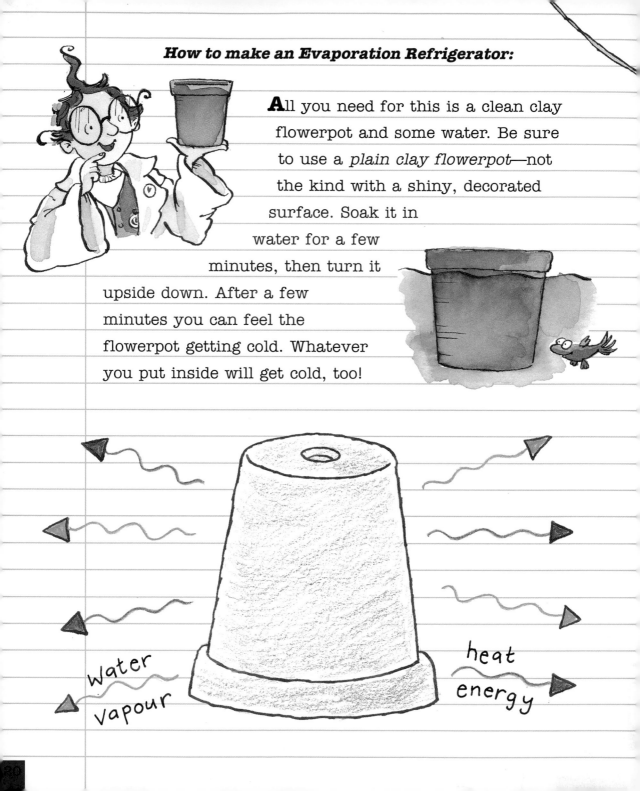

Water
vapour

heat
energy

HOW IT WORKS:

When water is exposed to the air, it slowly changes from a liquid to an invisible gas called water vapor. This change is called evaporation. When you hang wet clothing on a clothesline, the water in the clothing evaporates—it turns into water vapor. When water evaporates from the clay surface, it soaks up heat energy, cooling the flowerpot and the glass of milk.

You can feel the same thing happen on your skin when you sweat. The sweat evaporates and cools your skin.

Now, said the professor, "Its time to clean."

"You want me to help wash the dishes?" I asked.

"No! said the professor. "We are going to clean some water!"

CLEANING WATER WITH A TOWEL

The professor led me out into his garden and showed me a big mud puddle. He scooped up a glass of the brown water.

"What do you see?" he asked.

"A glass full of brown water."

"Precisely!" said the professor. "Now, I'm going to make this water turn clear!" We went back into the house and, using an empty glass, a few books, and a strip of towel, the professor set up a strange-looking experiment.

HOW TO MAKE MUDDY WATER CLEAR:

1. Put the glass of muddy water on top of a pile of books.

The pile should be higher than the empty glass.

2. Set the empty glass on the table.

3. Put one end of the strip of towel into the muddy water.

4. Hang the other end of the towel in the empty glass.

We watched for a few minutes, but nothing happened.

"It might take a while," the professor said. "Why don't you come back tomorrow?" Since we had eaten all the cookies, I went home. The next day I returned. The glass that had been filled with muddy water was dry.

But the glass that had been empty was full of clear water!

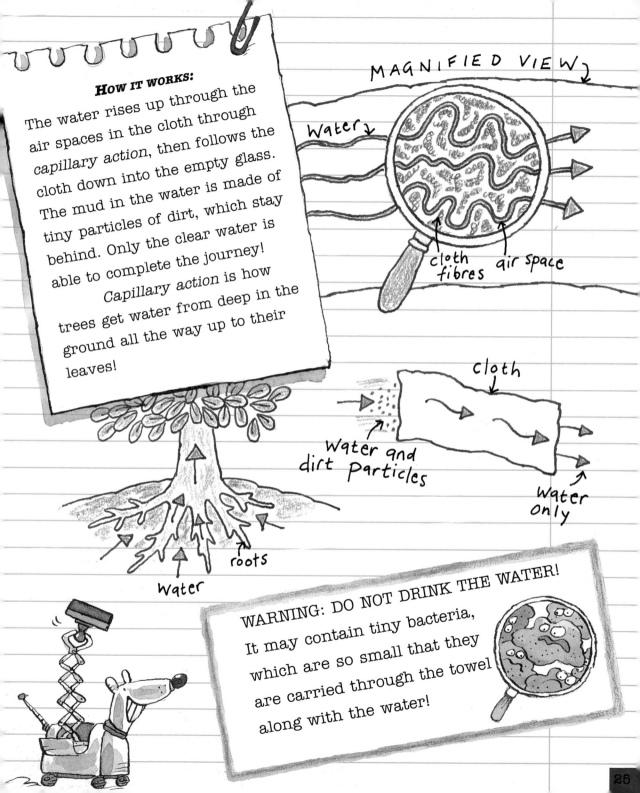

HOW IT WORKS:

The water rises up through the air spaces in the cloth through capillary action, then follows the cloth down into the empty glass. The mud in the water is made of tiny particles of dirt, which stay behind. Only the clear water is able to complete the journey!

Capillary action is how trees get water from deep in the ground all the way up to their leaves!

MAGNIFIED VIEW

Water

cloth fibres   air space

cloth

water and dirt particles

water only

roots

Water

WARNING: DO NOT DRINK THE WATER! It may contain tiny bacteria, which are so small that they are carried through the towel along with the water!

CARVING THROUGH SOLID ROCK

"**O**kay," I said as I munched on a cookie, "you've made steel and clay float. You've made a magnifying glass out of water. And you've made a refrigerator out of a wet flowerpot! What's next?"

"Now we use water to carve through solid rock! This is called *erosion.* This is how the Grand Canyon was made." The professor went out to his back yard. He propped the end of his garden hose against a big rock, then turned on the water so that a thin dribble ran down the side of the rock.

"How long is this going to take?" I asked.

The professor looked at his watch. "About ten thousand years," he said.

"I don't think I can wait that long."

The professor laughed. "You are so impatient!" He settled into a comfortable lawnchair to wait.

After a while, I got tired of watching and went home. As far as I know, Professor Solomon Snickerdoodle is still out there, trying to make another Grand Canyon!

HOW EROSION WORKS:
When water passes over rock, it slowly dissolves the minerals that bind the rock together. Tiny bits of rock break away and are carried away by the running water.

The Grand Canyon was carved by water. For tens of thousands of years, the Colorado River slowly wore away the rock and soil. Today, the Grand Canyon is over one mile deep!

$$C = mc^2$$

$$\begin{array}{r} 11 \\ \times 5 \\ \hline 55 \end{array}$$

$$a^2 + b^2 = c^2$$

$$\frac{1}{2}bh = \text{area of triangle}$$